HAZZELELPONI

Deliver Me, O God, Who Regards Me

John E. Harrison, MDiv.

Good Tidings

Copyright © 2024 John Harrison

All rights reserved.

ISBN: 979-8-218-46034-1

Dedication: This book is dedicated to Pastor Fredi Vega, a wonderful preacher and teacher of God's Word. He taught on how to read God's Word so that it comes alive for us. It is to this end, and him, that this book is dedicated. Thank you!

Scripture: These were the sons of the father of Etam: Jezreel, Ishma, and Idbash. The name of their sister was Hazzelelponi. 1 Chronicles 4:3.

Note: The World English Bible Version is used throughout this book, unless noted otherwise.

Preface: *Hazzelelponi. What a curious name! It is a rather long name, and it ends in a vowel, which makes it a fitting name for a woman. Her name is mentioned in God's Word, but her mother's name is not. But imagine with me for just a moment, how her mother could have used that name if her daughter was in trouble. That name would carry! Hazzelelponi-iiiiiiiii*

I invite you to join me on an adventure together. Hazzelelponi!

Put your walking shoes on and let's go! I'll wait.

Introduction: The Search

I live near the New Hampshire Seacoast. I have lived near the ocean for most of my life. A favorite activity of mine is to walk along the beach, searching for treasures. There are a lot of natural treasures to be found, even for the casual beach walker. It only takes a little bit of time and a good pair of legs, a keen eye, and a spot of energy.

There are lots of seashell fragments to be seen along the beach, most of which, although interesting for the beginning collector or observer, are best left to lay there to be washed back out to sea. With a little bit of patience, the searcher will spot the occasional whole seashell. They have been well polished by the seemingly endless washing back and forth, up the beach and back out to sea again. They will be pretty and colorful. The keeper shells will be missing the critter that once inhabited the shell, as those that are occupied will soon produce an undesirable odor, once removed from their water supply. Those are best left to return to their ocean habitat.

What I am looking for, as I traverse the beach, is commonly known as the sand dollar. Its name well describes its appearance. It will be sandy in color and shaped like a silver dollar coin. The most common appearances are fragments, bits and pieces, or those that are missing a piece. The object of my search is for a whole sand dollar, absent of that critter which once occupied its disc, and washed clean by the surf. Interestingly though, if the sand dollar were to be broken open, one would find a treasure within it. There are five pieces within it, shaped like doves. The count of five doves matches the star-shaped design on the surface of the sand dollar, as it has what is called five ray symmetry. The star has five arms and there are five doves within the sand dollar.

I am not the only one of God's creatures who does this. I have observed squirrels in my front yard looking for food under the snow in the winter. They seem to know that there is something under there that is worth finding. They look and sniff and dig, and they look and sniff and dig.

And then they'll find something of interest and value in their search, they'll put it in their cheeks, they'll look some more, and eventually, they'll scurry across the yard, scamper up a tree, and cherish their big find!

So, what does all of this have to do with our story? You may well ask. It is more than just an interesting introduction.

I read the Bible, present tense, the Word of God, in the same way. There are treasures to be found within the Book that our God has given us to read. The casual reader will be likely to gloss or glide right over some of the best treasures.

Like a second walk back down the same beach, the seasoned reader of God's Word will spot treasures laying along the path that were not likely noticed when reading through for the first time, or the second, or even the third, or fourth, or fifth read.

Like my dear pastime of walking the beach, I have been reading God's Word more than just casually, since I was thirteen years of age, reading it through, to the best of my knowledge, about once a year, for an estimate of about fifty-two times, as of this writing. It was on this, the fifty-second read, that I spotted the name Hazzelelponi. The woman's name had been laying there, during all of my previous reads, and I had passed over it, unnoticed, along with a bevy of other names that are probably of similar interest to another searcher of God's Word. But on this, my latest read, the name Hazzelelponi smiled up at me and called out to me, to be picked up and noticed, read over carefully, and discovered anew.

Where did I get the idea to read the Bible this way? Wasn't reading it through once good enough? Then I could say that I had read the Bible. That's what I used to think. I used to carry one back and forth to church with me, every Sunday, religiously. I would read along with the Sunday school lesson at church. That was reading the Bible, right? I got enough at church. Eventually if I went to church long enough, I would read through the whole Bible, and then I could say that I had read it.

Well one day, a couple of teenage girls at church asked me what would happen to me if I got into a car accident on the way home from church and died. What would happen to me? Where would I go? Where would I spend eternity? They gave me something to think about that night and I gave it a lot of thought. Then one night, I knelt beside my bed and prayed a real prayer for the first time in my life, not that 'Now I lay me down to sleep...' kind of prayer, a real prayer. I told God that I was sorry for my sins and that I wanted to know this God and the Lord that these girls had told me about that night. To make a long story short, before this becomes what this book is about instead of Hazzelelponi's story, God forgave me of my sins, the Lord came to live in my heart, and I experienced: deliver me, O God, Who regards me.

Some time later, God spoke to my heart, and I felt like He wanted me to become a minister in a church. I thought: "Really, God? Me?" Well, my dear grandmother told me one day that she could see me standing behind a pulpit in a church, preaching a sermon. That confirmed it for me. I answered the call, went off to college, earned a Bachelor of Arts degree in religion, and then went on to seminary. It was there that the professors began to teach how to really read a passage of Scripture in the Bible.

They told me, "Read it, then read it again, then read it again, and again. When you think that you've gotten everything out of it that there is to get, read it again!" I began to read It that way. As I did, what they said would happen actually happened! The passage of Scripture came alive for me. I saw something in it that I had never seen before. I learned something new. There was something in that passage of Scripture that came alive for me and jumped right off the page!

"Isn't My Word like fire?" says the Lord. Jeremiah 23:29.

For the Word of God is living and active, and sharper than any two-edged sword, piercing even to the dividing of soul and

spirit, of both joints and marrow, and is able to discern the thoughts and intentions of the heart. Hebrews 4:12.

It was in this spirit that I read 1 Chronicles 4. I was reading a genealogy, one of those long, otherwise boring lists of begats, when I read this.

These were the sons of the father of Etam: Jezreel, Ishma, and Idbash. The name of their sister was Hazzelelponi. 1 Chronicles 4:3.

"Hazzelelponi!" It called out to me. "I am your search for today. I am life! I have meaning! Tell my story!"

Here it is, then, the story of Hazzelelponi! I invite you to read and enjoy it with me.

CHAPTER ONE: MEANING AND PRONUNCIATION

Hers is a Hebrew name. She was a woman of Jewish heritage and Jewish faith. Her name, translated from the Hebrew language to our English language, has two possible meanings: deliver me, O God Who regards me (or regardeth me, for the King James reader), or the deliverance of the God Who regards me (or regardeth me).

Her name will likely appear strange, or awkward, to most English readers. It will likely not sound fitting as a good name for most women. However, the name ends with a vowel, making it a female name for a lot of languages. The seasoned reader of the Bible will likely notice the Sacred Name El, positioned in the middle of the name. This is the Hebrew Name for God. It will actually seem to appear twice within the name. However, the first appearance is the ending of the first part of the name, Hazzel, meaning deliver me. The name Hazzel may also appear in some translations of the Bible with just one letter z, as Hazel, from which we get our English woman's name, Hazel.

The ending of the name Hazzelelponi is, of course, poni. It can mean either second-born child, or second daughter. The last letter is a long I, pronounced as 'eye' or together as pawn-eye, or perhaps more smoothly and correctly, as po-nye. The three names then, are broken up as Hazzel-el-poni. When we put all three of these names together, we have the name of this Hebrew woman: Hazzelelponi.

Herein, we have gained a quick look at this otherwise strange sounding, and seemingly awkward looking name of Hazzelelponi. May God guide us as we take a look together at this treasure from His Word.

CHAPTER TWO: HAZZEL

Here we have the first part of this woman's name: Hazzel. The name means: deliver me.

The name also appears in some translations of the Bible with only one z, as Hazelelponi. As such, the name means a shade or shadow, which seems to imply that the shade turned towards me, and hints toward a hope of Divine protection and assurance. This meaning is seen in the 121st Psalm.

The Lord is your Keeper. The Lord is your Shade on your right hand. Psalm 121:5.

We also see this meaning in the 91st Psalm.

He who dwells in the secret place of the Most High will rest in the Shadow of the Almighty. Psalm 91:1.

We see the meaning of shadow in the 36th Psalm.

How precious is your loving kindness, God! The children of men take refuge under the Shadow of Your Wings. Psalm 36:7.

We also see this meaning in the story of Lot in Sodom.

**"Don't do anything to these men, because they have come under the shadow of my roof."
Genesis 19:8.**

The prefix Hazzel means deliver me. An example of this may be found in the 43rd Psalm.

Vindicate me, God, and plead my cause against an ungodly nation. Oh, deliver me from deceitful and wicked men. Psalm 43:1.

We also see this meaning in a plea from David to Saul.

May the Lord therefore be judge, and give sentence between me and you, and see, and plead my cause, and deliver me out of your hand. 1 Samuel 24:15.

Hazzel, the first part of this woman's name then, means to be under the shade, or shadow, of Divine protection and assurance. This woman has a blessing in her name. God must have been her Divine protection.

Can we picture being under the shadow of Divine protection? Consider Boaz's words of comfort to Ruth.

"May the Lord repay your work, and a full reward be given to you from the Lord, the God of Israel, under Whose Wings you have come to take refuge." Ruth 2:12.

Or the words of the Psalmist:

Hide me under the shadow of Your Wings. Psalm 17:8.

Or the Words of the Lord:

"How often I would have gathered your children together, even as a hen gathers her chicks under her wings." Matthew 23:37.

Commentary

I was told this story about the name Hazzelelponi.

Andrew: "I met a young lady named Hazel & told her: 'You're the prettiest Hazel I've ever met."

Hazel: "Let me guess: I'm the only Hazel you've ever met."

Andrew: "No!"

Hazel: "You've met someone else named Hazel."

Andrew: "Yes, I went to church with a woman named Hazel."

Hazel: "Was she ugly?"

Andrew: "Well, she was in her '90s so it's hard to tell. She may have been pretty in her day."

Hazel: "So what you're trying to say is I'm prettier than a 90-year-old woman."

Andrew: "Actually, at this point, I'm trying to say as little as possible as I've clearly dug a hole for myself."

Hazel: "I'm aware that people think of 'Hazel' as an old lady name, but my mom named me after a woman in the Bible."

Andrew: "I'm not aware of any Hazels in the Bible."

Hazel: "She said her name was longer & began with 'Hazel', but no one's ever been able to find it for me."

Andrew: "It shouldn't be difficult. If you give me your e-mail address, I'll summarize what the Bible has to say about your namesake."

Hazel: "I don't know if you're trying to help me or if this is the lamest pick-up line ever."

Andrew (to wife): "Millie, this is Hazel. Her mom told her she's named after a woman in the Bible whose name begins with 'Hazel', but she can't figure out who it is, and I offered to help."

Andrew (to Hazel): "Hazel, this is my wife of 25 years, Millie."

Millie: "If there's a woman in the Bible named Hazel, he'll find it for you, and you can trust him."

I enjoyed that story. Thank you for letting me share it with you.

I would have thought that it would have been easier to cite famous women named Hazel that most people would know, but there just do not seem to be any. There was a television show named Hazel, which aired for 5 seasons in the 1960s, which starred Shirley Booth as Hazel Burke. Otherwise, the most famous people named Hazel seem to hail from the United Kingdom. Topping this list is Hazel Blears, the former chair of the Labor Party of the UK. Next in line seems to be Hazel O'Connor, a British songwriter and actress, famous for her early 1980s hit single, "Eighth Day."

Otherwise, the origin for the name Hazel seems to be connected to the hazelnut, from the hazel tree. It could also be from our old English word haesel, which refers to the light brown color. Famous women with hazel eyes include: Demi Moore, Tyra Banks, Angelina Jolie, and Jennifer Garner.

CHAPTER THREE: HAZEL

There is an alternate spelling then, for the first part of our woman's name: Hazel. As such, the name means: God sees. There are only a few occurrences of such in the Bible. One such occurrence is found in the story of Abram and Sarai (later named Abraham and Sarah) and Hagar. Sarai was barren and could not bear a child to Abram. They were growing old and out of desperation, Sarai formulated a plan to give her handmaiden, Hagar, to Abram as a second wife, so that he could go in to her, and the resulting child would be counted as hers. Abram agreed and they proceeded as planned. When Hagar immediately became pregnant, Sarai despised Hagar and treated her harshly. Hagar then fled from Sarai into the wilderness. The Lord's Angel found her by a well of water and asked her where she was from and where she was going. When Hagar explained her situation, the Lord's Angel told her to return to Sarai. He further told her that He would greatly increase her offspring, as she would bear a son, and that she was to call his name Ishmael, as the Lord had heard her affliction. Astonished that she was allowed to see God and live, she then called the Name of the Lord Who had spoken to her: "You Are A God Who Sees."

She called the name of the Lord Who spoke to her, "You are a God Who Sees." Genesis 16:13.

Much later in their story, after God changed the elderly couple's names to Abraham and Sarah, and after they had a son named Isaac, a dispute arose during a weaning party for Isaac. Sarah told

Abraham to cast out the woman, Hagar, and her son, Ishmael. Hagar found herself in the wilderness, her food and water exhausted. She set the boy under a bush in the shade and sat down to cry. God heard her cry, and opened her eyes so that she could see the well of water near where she was sitting, and she gave the boy a drink. The God Who Sees heard her cry and opened her eyes, allowing her to see.

God opened her eyes, and she saw a well of water. She went, filled the container with water, and gave the boy a drink. Genesis 21:19.

Incidentally, it is interesting to note here, that God meets women either by a well, or by a spring of water. God meets women in their routine of life, such as gathering water for the family. God also meets women in their time of distress, in which they seek solace alongside a source of water.

The story of Hazzelelponi, then, is connected to the story of Hagar. Within the name of Hazzelelponi is the alternate spelling of Hazel, meaning God sees.

Commentary

The story is told of a woman and her husband who were searching for a name for their baby. They were having difficulty conceiving, underwent fertility treatments, and even suffered a miscarriage. After crying out to God in despair, they were later enabled to conceive and became pregnant with a baby girl.

As they were searching for a name for their baby, the woman came across the name Hazel and learned that the name meant 'God sees.' Further, she came across the name Hazzelelponi in the Bible and learned about the connection to the name Hazel, being derived from the Hebrew word Hazael, meaning God sees.

The woman was touched and encouraged by the story of Hagar, who was visited by the Lord's Angel, Who saw Hagar's distress and gave her a precious promise from God. The woman was further touched by the second half of Hagar's story, whom God heard in her distress and enabled her to see the well of water to give her child a drink.

The woman was so moved by these stories and the meaning of the names, that she and her husband decided to name their girl Hazel. God saw their distress, met their need, and enabled them to have a child.

Hazzelelponi then, contains the name Hazel, in its alternate spelling, which means God sees. God sees us in our times of distress and meets our needs. Thank You, Lord!

CHAPTER FOUR: EL (GOD)

Here we have the second part of this woman's name. Hazzel-Elponi. El was an early Name for God.

El was the God whom the Hebrew patriarchs worshipped. El was the first half of a two-part Name, for instance: El Shaddai, or God Almighty; El Elyon, or God Most High; and El Elohe, or the God of Israel. God later revealed Himself to Moses as Yahweh, or I AM.

Hazzelelponi was a woman of an el-ite group of people in the Bible who had the name for God within their name. She bore this name in the very middle of her name, as: Deliver me, O God, Who regards me.

Some other members of this el-ite group are:

NAME = MEANING:

Daniel = God is my Judge.
Eleazar = God has helped.
Eli = My God.
Eliab = God is my Father.
Eliakim = God will establish.
Eliezer = God is my help.
Elihu = My God is He.
Elijah = The Lord is my God.
Elimilech = My God is kind.
Eliphaz = My God is pure gold.

Elisha = God is salvation.
Elishama = God hears.
Elisheba = God is my oath.
Elizabeth = God is my oath.
Elkanah = God has purchased.
Gabriel = God is my strength.
Israel (Jacob) = Struggle, or Prince, with God
Joel = The Lord is God.
Michael = Who is like God?
Nathaniel = Given by God.
Samuel = God has heard.

Other el words in the Bible

WORD = MEANING:

Elbow = Having the capacity for radical change in direction.
Elder = Of greater age.
Election = Chosen by God.
Elements = The first part of anything
Eleven = Almost twelve; imperfect; chaos.
Eloquent = Giving a clear, strong message.
Elevation = Raising to a higher place.

El means either God, or power, in the Hebrew language. As we've seen, it appears often in Biblical names, as well as in the Hebrew language, both ancient and modern. The appearance of 'el' in names around the globe shows the influence that the Bible has had on our world.

Our God is: the God Who regards me. Thank You, Lord!

CHAPTER FIVE: PONI

Here we have the ending of this woman's name. Hazzel-el-Poni.

Since her name again means: The God Who regards me, the ending of her name means that she is regarded. That means that she was looked upon or thought of with a particular or special feeling. That makes her as special as her name appears.

When God finished with His grand Creation, He looked upon all that He had made and saw that it was good, even very good.

God saw everything that He had made, and, behold, it was very good. Genesis 1:31.

On the flip side of that coin, God later looked upon the Earth and saw that it was corrupt.

God saw the Earth, and saw that it was corrupt, for all flesh had corrupted their way on the Earth. Genesis 6:12.

Even later, God looked down upon the Hebrew people wandering in the wilderness, He regarded their groaning, and remembered His covenant with Abraham, Isaac, and Jacob.

God saw the children of Israel, and God was concerned about them. Exodus 2:25.

Further, God regards, or looks upon, our hearts.

The Lord looks at the heart. 1 Samuel 16:7.

Despite the fact that God regards, or looks upon us, we cannot look upon God.

The Lord said, "You cannot see my face and live." Exodus 33:20.

Hazzelelponi, then, had a special ending on her name. God regarded her, or looked upon her, or thought of her, with a particular, or special feeling. She was special to God!

Special! The best gift that God ever gave man was woman. When God made man, He reached down, scooped up a handful of dirt, formed it into a man, and breathed into it the breath of life. God then regarded man, or looked upon him, and said that it was not good for man to be alone.

A search was made for a suitable partner for man, but none was found. God's solution was to create woman. But, when God created woman, He didn't use dirt. He put man into a deep sleep, He removed a rib from his side, and made woman from man. Then He gave her to him as his wife. And man was pleased!

The Lord God formed man from the dust of the ground, and breathed into his nostrils the breath of life; and man became a living soul. The Lord God said, "It is not good for man to be alone. I will make him a helper comparable to him. But for man there was not found a helper comparable to him. The Lord God caused man to fall into a deep sleep. As the man slept, He took one of his ribs, and closed up the flesh in its place. The Lord God made a woman from the rib which He had taken from the man, and brought her to the man. The man said, "This is now bone of my bones, and flesh of my flesh." Genesis 2:7, 18, and 20-23.

Poni means second child, or second daughter. She had at least three siblings. Three brothers are named: Jezreel, Ishma, and Idbash. The meaning of her name may indicate that she was the second born among these children. One of her brothers may have been the first born, she may have come next, and two brothers may have followed. She may have been the second daughter. She may have had an unnamed sister, who may have come along somewhere within the birth order, and preceded Hazzelelponi.

Granted, this is conjecture, or extrapolating a supposition from the meaning of her name. However, one thing is certain: there was something special about her. She was named in Scripture, a rare honor for a woman of her time.

Hazzelelponi had a good beginning. God sees. She centered well. God. She ended with a special ending. God regards, me. Of all people, God regarded Hazzelelponi, a Biblical woman, of whom really very little is actually known. God took this woman, born to three brothers, and made her special.

God takes those of whom the world thinks of as less, and makes them special. 1 Corinthians 1:27. (My paraphrase)

CHAPTER SIX. OF THE TRIBE OF JUDAH

We know that Hazzelelponi was of the tribe of Judah. Her name appears in a list of those belonging to, or born into, the tribe of Judah. This in itself makes her special.

The sons of Judah. 1 Chronicles 4:1.

The tribe of Judah was one of the twelve tribes of Israel. Their tribe was named after Judah, who was the son of Jacob (later named Israel), who, in turn, was the son of Isaac, who, in turn, was the son of Abraham, the patriarch of Israel. The tribe of Judah became the most powerful and the most important of all the tribes of Israel. They produced the mighty kings known as David and Solomon. Most importantly, the Messiah was prophesied to come from the tribe of Judah. Their tribe is represented by a lion, as when Jacob blessed Judah on his deathbed, he called him a "lion's whelp" or cub.

Judah is a lion's cub. Genesis 49:9.

The tribe of Judah, along with Benjamin, was allowed to return to Jerusalem after the captivity. That fact allowed the Jewish people to survive and continue, and gave the people their name today: Jews, or Jewish, from Judah.

Then, the heads of fathers' households of Judah and Benjamin, the priests, and the Levites, all whose spirit God had stirred to go up rose up to build the Lord's house which is in Jerusalem. Ezra 1:5-6.

The tribe of Judah was the praise tribe, as Judah means "praise." While the Hebrew people were in the wilderness, the tribe of Judah would lead the other tribes, going out first, whenever they moved to a new location. After arriving in Canaan, the Promised Land, the tribe of Judah led the other tribes into battle. The tribe of Judah always went out first, wherever they went, since praise leads God's people into those things that are new in God.

The children of Israel arose, went up to Bethel, and asked counsel of God. They asked, "Who shall go up for us first to battle?" The Lord said, "Judah first." Judges 20:18.

Judah means praise because when Leah, Judah's mother, was giving birth, she praised the Lord. The Hebrew word for praise is: "yadah" which is close to Judah.

Leah conceived again, and bore a son. She said, "This time I will praise the Lord." Therefore she named him Judah. Genesis 29:35.

So, the next time that you hear someone say, "Yada, yada, yada" they just may be giving praise!

Judah was an interceder.

When Joseph's brothers wanted to sell him into slavery out of jealousy and hatred, Judah interceded and convinced them not to do so. He interceded for Joseph's life.

Judah said to his brothers, "What profit is it if we kill our brother and conceal his blood? Come, let our hand not be on him, for he is our brother, our flesh." Genesis 37:26-27.

Judah was a negotiator, who convinced Jacob (Israel), his father, to let him take his brother, Benjamin, back to Joseph in Egypt.

Judah said to Israel, his father, "Send the boy with me, and we'll get up and go, so that we may live, and not die." Genesis 43:8.

The tribe of Judah remained loyal to the house of David after the nation of Israel split into two kingdoms.

There was no one who followed David's house, except for the tribe of Judah only. 1 Kings 12:20.

Hazzelelponi then, was listed among those belonging to the tribe of Judah. This fact makes her special!

CHAPTER SEVEN: FAMILY

Amazingly, we now know more about Hazzelelponi than we know about the rest of her family. Her father's name was Etam, who was likely a descendant of Hur. She had three brothers: Jezreel, Ishma, and Idbash.

Etam is a fitting name for their father. The name means: "their covering."

Jezreel is the first brother listed. His name comes from two separate Hebrew words: "to sow" and "almighty." Therefore, his name means: "God will sow." Perhaps Jezreel fathered many children.

Ishma is the second brother listed. His name means: "desolate," "devastated," "abandoned," or "an empty place." Perhaps he was the second born and got less attention than the firstborn, had no children, or became abandoned. The meaning of his name is certainly less pleasant.

Idbash is the third brother listed. His name could have two possible meanings, one good and one bad, either: "flowing with honey" or "land of destruction." For his sake, let's hope it was the former. Perhaps he settled in a fertile land.

Otherwise, we know almost nothing else about Hazzelelponi's family. They were of the tribe of Judah, as previously mentioned, and were likely descended from Hur.

Hur, interestingly enough, was the firstborn of Ephrathah, the father of Bethlehem. This means that Ephrathah was the mother of Hur. Caleb, Hur's father, was the husband of Ephrathah. Hur had four sons: Uri, Shobal, Salma, and Hareph. The three latter brothers, sons of Uri, founded cities. Salma founded the city of Bethlehem, making Hur the father of Bethlehem.

These are the sons of Hur, the firstborn of Ephrathah, the father of Bethlehem. 1 Chronicles 4:4b.

This explains the prophecy.

But you, Bethlehem Ephrathah, being small among the clans of Judah, out of you one will come out to me that is to be ruler in Israel, whose goings out are from of old, from ancient times. Micah 5:2.

The genealogy continues on from there, listing many men, being sons and fathers. A notable reference is the name of Ashhur, the father of Tekoa, who had two wives, named Helah and Naarah.

The genealogy is interrupted to reference a man named Jabez, who has received much attention. He is given two whole verses and called honorable, or at least more so than his brothers. He called on the God of Israel, and requested a blessing, along with the enlargement of his border. He further asked for God's Hand to be upon him and to be kept from evil, that he may not cause pain. God granted his request.

The genealogy then continues on for many more verses. In the midst of it all, we found our Hazzelelponi!

CHAPTER EIGHT: TZELAFON

There is an yet another alternate spelling for our lady's name. It is: Zelelponith. As such, there is a village in Israel which may be named after her. Its name is Tzelafon.

Tzelafon is a moshav, or a village, in Israel. It is located to the north of Beit Shemesh, which, in turn, is a city in Israel, which is located about 19 miles west of Jerusalem, the newly declared capital of Israel, in the Jerusalem District of Israel. Tzelafon is much smaller, in 2022 it had a population of 1,095. Tzelafon was established in the year 1950, by people immigrating from Yemen. Previously, the land was known as Bayt Jiz, a depopulated village of Palestine. It is located on the western foothills of the Jerusalem Heights. More immigrants arrived from Morocco, in the year 1955.

Tzelafon is significant to our story, as we look back upon our calendar, as the years began to creep up upon the middle of the 20th century, specifically, as the 1940s began to come to a close. On November 29, 1947, the United Nations passed the UN Partition Plan, establishing a Jewish state in British Mandatory Palestine. This caused Arab countries to become hostile toward its Jewish citizens. Yemen, an Arab nation, also exhibited such hostilities. One month after the declaration, riots broke out in Aden, a major city in Yemen. More than 70 Jews in Yemen were killed, and the Jewish Quarter in Aden was burned and looted. Jews in Yemen were desperate to escape to the Jewish state. The Egyptian government moved to thwart such activity, blocking southern access points to the new Jewish state. The Red Sea and the Suez

Canal were blocked.

In further developments, on May 14, 1948, the head of the Jewish Agency, David Ben-Gurion, declared Israel to be a new and sovereign state. Then President of the United States of America Harry S. Truman, recognized Israel as a new nation on the same day.

With this declaration, David Ben-Gurion became the first prime minister of Israel. He appealed to other heads of state to assist in relocating the Jews in Yemen to the safety of the new state of Israel. This plea gave birth to an airlift operation funded by the American Jewish Joint Distribution Committee. Alaska Airlines played a role in the operation. They modified their planes to carry more passengers, replacing seats with benches and adding extra fuel tanks. The operation was dubbed 'On Wings of Eagles', and flights continued for almost one and a half years. Passengers flew on 'iron birds', with some Jewish people believing that they really were on the wings of eagles. Some recalled the exodus out of Egypt, into the Wilderness of Sinai, and the words which the Lord spoke to Moses, "You have seen what I did to the Egyptians, and how I bore you on eagles' wings, and brought you to myself." Exodus 19:4.

Others cited another 'eagles wings' passage.

Those who wait for the Lord will renew their strength. They will mount up with wings like eagles. They will run, and not be weary. They will walk, and not faint. Isaiah 40:31.

Although they had seen planes and knew what they were, they were overwhelmed with their redemption. They believed it to be a literal fulfillment of the wings of eagles prophecy.

The operation brought many Jews from Yemen into the village that would be named Tzelafon, after our lady, Hazzelelponi, or more accurately in this case, after the alternate spelling of her name: Zeleponith. God had regarded the Jews of Yemen, true to our lady's name, Hazzelelponi, the God Who Regards Me.

CHAPTER NINE: TZALAF

Tzelafon may also have been named after Capparis bushes, called Tzalaf, in the Hebrew language. The bushes have simple leaves, as well as petals and berries for fruit. It is a climbing shrub with branches, which also have spines for protection. It is a naturally growing shrub. Its flowers are small and white, which fade to either pink or purple. There are between 2 to 6 flowers in each row, which often develop before the leaves do. The bushes are mostly used by man for their fruit, which are high in nutrients. The bush's flower buds are also used for food. They are pickled and used as a vegetable condiment. Further uses for the bushes are: in landscaping, as they help to stop land erosion, and to attract butterflies. Other food source uses for the bushes are their fruits and seeds which are enjoyed by such as: birds, lizards, and caterpillars. Some species of the bushes are becoming rare, mostly due to the destruction of their habitat, and some are in danger of extinction.

These Capparis bushes then, are adorned with flowers and are protected with spines. God made them beautiful and provided for their protection. How appropriate then! Tzelafon may have named after our lady and the bushes may have been named after her village. Like our lady, they are special! They are beautiful and they are protected.

Tzelafon then, is a village in Israel, which was founded in 1950, and was named after Zelelponith, a variant name for Hazzelelponi.

CHAPTER TEN: A SECOND HAZZELELPONI

Although her name does not appear in Scripture, with our aforementioned Hazzelelponi being the only woman listed with that name, Rabbinic Jewish tradition tells us that there was another woman by that name.

Manoah's wife, who is also referred to as the mother of Samson in the book of Judges, is unnamed. She was a barren woman to whom the Angel of the Lord appears and is told that she will bear a son.

There was a certain man of Zorah, of the family of the Danites, whose name was Manoah; and his wife was barren, and childless. The Lord's angel appeared to the woman, and said to her, "See now, you are barren and childless; but you shall conceive and bear a son. Judges 13:2-3.

The woman then went and told her husband.

Then the woman came and told her husband, saying, "A man of God came to me, and his face was like the face of the angel of God, very awesome. I didn't ask him where he was from, neither did he tell me his name; but he said to me, 'Behold, you shall conceive and bear a son.'" Judges 13:6-7.

Manoah prayed to the Lord for guidance as to how to raise the child. The Lord listened to Manoah and appeared again to his wife, in the field where she sat.

God listened to the voice of Manoah, and the angel of God came again to the woman as she sat in the field; but Manoah, her husband, wasn't with her. Judges 13:9.

The woman ran and told her husband and they returned to the field together. They prepared a burnt offering of a young goat and offered it on a rock to the Lord. The Angel said that His Name was Wonderful.

As they watched, the Angel ascended toward the sky in the flame of the altar. They were afraid that they would die, as they had seen the Lord. The woman then voiced faith in the Lord.

"If the Lord were pleased to kill us, He wouldn't have received a burnt offering and a meal offering at our hand, and He wouldn't have shown us all these things, nor would He have told us such things as these at this time." Judges 13:23.

The woman later gave birth to Samson.

The woman bore a son and named him Samson. The child grew, and the Lord blessed him. Judges 13:24.

Rabbinic Jewish tradition names this woman of faith as Hazzelelponi. It is unclear as to whether this is the same woman named in 1 Chronicles 4:3 or another woman.

Commentators differ on their opinion of the wife of Manoah. Some say that she was more perceptive than her husband, as she immediately sensed something special about the One Who appeared to her and that there was a divine purpose behind the appearance and the message that was given to her. Others portray the woman as somewhat cynical, commenting that she neither prayed for a child beforehand, nor did she pray for a meaning to the appearance at the time, whereas Manoah sought guidance from the Lord. The woman also did not praise God afterwards. She simply named him Samson and raised her son. Yet, whether or not Manoah's wife was our Hazzelelponi, one thing is sure - the Lord regarded, or looked upon her, and she was special!

CHAPTER ELEVEN: A THIRD HAZZELELPONI

Again, although she is not named in Scripture, Rabbinic Jewish tradition tells us that there is yet another woman by this name.

The name of Samson's first wife is not mentioned in Scripture; however, she also may have been called either Hazzelelponi, or a variant of that name, Zelelponith. Her mother's name was Etam and her sister was named Ishma. She was a daughter of the Philistines, whom Samson met in Timnah.

Samson went down to Timnah, and saw a woman in Timnah of the daughters of the Philistines. Judges 14:1.

He went and told his parents about her and asked them to get her for him as a wife. This displeased them, as she was an uncircumcised Philistine. Nevertheless, Samson was well pleased with her and took her as his wife.

He went down and talked with the woman, and she pleased Samson well. After a while he returned to take her. Judges 14:7-8.

Samson and his wife later argued over a riddle that he made. He also argued with local men over the riddle, as they enticed his wife to solve it for them. Samson gave in to violence, struck thirty of the men, and took their plunder. His wife was then given to another man, who had been his friend.

But Samson's wife was given to his companion, who had been his

friend. Judges 14:20.

Samson's first wife then, must certainly be a different woman, who happened to bear the name of Hazzelelponi. Curiously, she may have had the same name as Samson's mother.

CHAPTER TWELVE: CONCLUSION

Through it all, we have hopefully experienced the joy of looking for treasures within God's Word. We have seen within the curious name of Hazzelelponi, a special woman. She was looked upon and regarded by God as special. She was named in Scripture, whereas many other women, perhaps even a majority, were not named. She was perhaps the second child, and maybe even the second daughter, within a family of three brothers. She belonged to the tribe of Judah, the praise tribe, which went out first, by the command of the Lord God. She was special!

Women: you are special! You are specially created by God! You are looked upon and regarded by God! In your times of distress, expect God to look down upon you and see you, even in your routine matters of life. Expect God to see you, hear your cries of distress, and meet your needs. Expect God to use you in a special and unique way in His plan for Your life.

"For I know the thoughts that I think toward you," says the Lord, "thoughts of peace, and not of evil, to give you hope and a future." Jeremiah 29:11.

Many, my God, are the wonderful works which You have done, and Your thoughts which are toward us. If I would declare and speak of them, they are more than can be counted. Psalm 40:5.

Men: let us stand by our women and love and support them. Let us go with them as they meet with the Lord. Let us be a comfort to them in their time of distress and listen to them. We are in this together.

Therefore a man will leave his father and his mother, and will join with his wife, and they will be one flesh. Genesis 2:24.

Let your spring be blessed. Rejoice in the wife of your youth. Proverbs 5:18.

Husbands, love your wives, even as Christ also loved the assembly, and gave Himself up for it. Ephesians 5:25.

Perhaps we are not the firstborn of our family and feel as though we are less important. Perhaps we are a second born child. Know that God takes those who are considered as less, looks upon them, regards them, and considers them as important, even special. He has a wonderful plan for our lives! Rejoice! We are children of God!

In the place where it was said to them, 'You are not my people,' they will be called 'sons of the living God.' Hosea 1:10.

But as many as received Him, to them He gave the right to become God's children, to those who believe in His Name. John 1:12.

Thank you for joining me on our journey! It has been a pleasure to have you along the way! May God bless you!

Blessings in parting, first to the Jew and then to the Gentile.

These are written that you may be blessed and take refuge in Him. Adapted from Psalm 2:12c.

These are written, that you may believe that Jesus is the Christ, the Son of God, and that believing you may have life in His Name. John 20:31.

Shalom! Maranatha!

About the author: John Harrison has a Bachelor of Arts degree in Religion and a Master of Divinity degree. John is a chaplain, a minister in an alternate setting, such as at a hospital. John attends church regularly and enjoys worshipping the Lord in song. John and his wife live near a lake, where John enjoys kayaking. They also live near the ocean, where John enjoys walking along the beach and hunting for shells and other such treasure. John is semi-retired and enjoys writing books in his free time.

www.ingramcontent.com/pod-product-compliance
Lightning Source LLC
Chambersburg PA
CBHW070047070426
42449CB00012BA/3179